God, Guns and Ulster

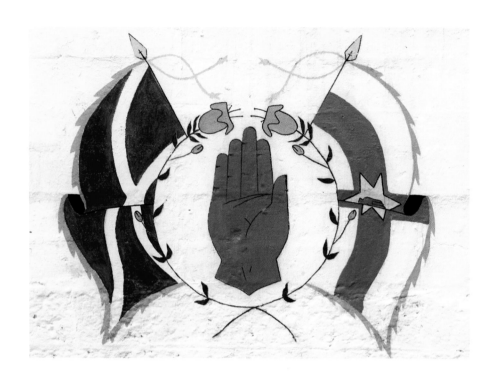

CAXTON EDITIONS

AN IMPRINT OF CAXTON PUBLISHING GROUP
20 BLOOMSBURY STREET, LONDON WC1 3QA

© CAXTON EDITIONS, 2003

ISBN 1 84067 536 5

A COPY OF THE CIP DATA IS AVAILABLE FROM THE
BRITISH LIBRARY UPON REQUEST

REPROGRAPHICS BY GA GRAPHICS
DESIGN BY POINTING DESIGN

PRINTED BY CTPS

PAGES 6 AND 7: UDA PARADE

God, Guns and Ulster

A History of Loyalist Paramilitaries

Text by Ian S Wood

CAXTON EDITIONS

CONTENTS

Belfast Boyne mural – The five pointed star is an important masonic symbol,
also used in Orange regalia.

Post card depicting King William of Orange landing at
Carrickfergus 14 June 1690.

CHAPTER ONE

EARLY ULSTER: WAR, PLANTATION, LOYALTY AND REBELLION

Emain Macha, or Navan in its Anglicised form, is one of Ireland's major archaeological sites. Three miles west of Armagh, the contours of its fortifications are still clear. It is likely to have been a religious and political capital of the Iron Age Uluti who gave their name to Ulaid, once a confederation of warrior kingdoms which in pre-Christian times covered much of the present area of Northern Ireland and in fact reached as far as the River Boyne.

High kings of Ireland gave tribute at Emain Macha and its stockades and defensive ditches were at the centre of Ulaid or Ulster resistance to raids and attacks by Celts from further west and south. One of the greatest of these was led by Queen Maeve of Connacht (or Connaught) to capture a renowned brown bull from the Uluti. An epic poem, dating possibly to the seventh century AD, 'The Cattle Raid of Cooley', describes how Maeve's warriors were foiled by Cu Chulainn, a legendary fighter. His bravery became a symbol of both Irish and Ulster resistance to invaders and occupiers. A sculpture of him occupies a place of honour in Dublin's General Post Office where the rebel republic was proclaimed in Easter Week of

1916, but his likeness now also adorns many paramilitary murals in Loyalist areas of Belfast.

Eventually the Celts broke Ulster's armies at the battle of Moira, in what is now County Down, in 637AD. Many survivors of this defeat fled to the Western Scottish kingdom of Dalriada. Whether or not they were the Cruthin people, with ethnic and cultural affinities to the Picts, has been hotly disputed. Some Ulster Loyalists, seeking amidst the turmoil of the last thirty years to define better their own identity, have claimed this and even described the early seventeenth century plantation of Ulster as 'the return of the Cruthin'

Whatever the truth or not of these assertions, the battle of Moira was hugely important, for the extinction of the Ulaid kingdom cleared the way for Ulster's later incorporation within the Anglo-Norman settlement of Ireland in the twelfth and thirteenth centuries. Ulster became an earldom which was granted to Hugh de Lacy in 1204. When he died without heirs others took over his title and built formidable castles like Carrickfergus and Dundrum to make a reality of their presence.

The siege of Derry in 1689.

It was a settlement rather than a conquest. Some great Ulster clans and their leaders fought on against English attempts to rule them; others, as elsewhere in Ireland, assimilated themselves to the settlers. When open rebellion flared up it was often led from Ulster. In August 1598, English forces suffered their greatest defeat in Ireland in the entire sixteenth century when one of their armies was ambushed and slaughtered at the Yellow Ford north of Armagh by an army led by the rebel Hugh O'Neill, Earl of Tyrone.

By then the English presence had, with the Reformation, brought Protestantism to the minority in Ireland who would accept it. Reinforcing their numbers, as well as securing English rule and civilizing 'barbaric' natives, was a reason for the policy of 'plantation', or creating new English and Scottish settlements.

This predates the reign of King James VI of Scotland and I of England, but his decision after the 1603 Union of the Crowns to give priority to an Ulster Plantation had huge consequences.

Plantation went ahead elsewhere on the island but by 1641, 15,000 English and Scottish Protestants had settled in Ulster, availing themselves of good land divided amongst them in baronies and precincts decided on and mapped out by the King's Lord Deputy, Sir Arthur Chichester and his advisers. Chichester, who as Governor of Carrickfergus had carried out ruthless 'scorched earth' measures against Catholic rebels in East Tyrone, took a more cautious view of plantation than the King and favoured re-granting of confiscated land to 'loyal' native Irish but the process had a momentum of its own. The great London-based trading corporations who were integral to it brought skilled workers over with them and by the time the War of the Three Kingdoms was launched in 1641 by Charles I and his Parliamentary opponents there was a Protestant garrison community in Ulster with a siege psychology which has never left it.

The massive walls of Londonderry, to be grimly tested in the great siege of 1689, still symbolise this mindset but events prior to that reinforced it dramatically, like the October 1641 rising led by the native Irish aristocracy against a Dublin administration which had come under Puritan control. This quickly became a murderous spasm of vengeance unleashed on the Protestant planter population by a land-hungry Catholic peasantry maddened by a sense of dispossession. Possibly 12,000 people died by fire, sword, the gallows and drowning as well as exposure and sickness after being driven from their homes in freezing weather.

As the historian Professor ATQ Stewart wrote: 'warning bonfires blazed from hilltop to hilltop, and beating drums summoned men to the defence of castles and walled towns crowded with refugees.' The massacres, notably in Portadown, burned themselves into folk memory. Cromwell subsequently crushed the rebel Irish and stepped up land confiscation and resettlement but the crisis induced by the accession in 1685 of the Catholic James VII of Scotland and II of England reignited Protestant fears.

James was overthrown by Parliament in November 1688 and replaced by his son-in-law William of Orange. James's cousin and ally, Louis XIV of France, urged him to use Ireland as a base from which to win back his crown. Much of it in fact was under his control at the moment of his flight from England for he had methodically filled the administration and army command there with Catholics.

When James landed in Ireland in March 1689 there was already panic among Ulster Protestants. In Londonderry the previous

December, thirteen apprentices had secured the gates of the city against an approaching Catholic army. Their action, celebrated by Loyalists in the city to this day every December, set the scene for a siege which began in April the following year after an attempt to surrender the city by its military commander Robert Lundy had been foiled. His name is still, for Ulster Protestants synonymous with treachery and his effigy is annually burned as part of the December commemorations.

The siege lasted for one hundred and five days during which the defenders of the city and its population suffered appallingly. Detailed accounts of the garrison's expenditure were kept and, as starvation worsened, they enumerate the going prices for the meat of cats, dogs, rats and mice as well as 'one quarter of a dog fattened by eating the bodies of slain Irish'. On 28 July two ships laden with food, broke the boom with which the Jacobites had blocked the Foyle estuary, effectively ending the siege. Fifteen thousand lives had been lost but the city's survival became central to a Protestant self image of defiance, symbolised by the 'brave thirteen' apprentice boys and the shouts of 'no surrender' from the walls which greeted King James's offer of terms to the garrison.

Events in Londonderry, followed the next year by William of Orange's equally symbolic victory over James's army at the Boyne, secured both a Protestant succession to the British crown and a Protestant ascendancy in Ireland. Ulster's planter population, much strengthened by new arrivals from England and Scotland, was part of this though the benefits were unequally shared. Many Presbyterians, Methodists and other religious dissenters resented the privileged position of the Irish Episcopal church and left in large numbers for the American colonies.

Large numbers of them supported the cause of American independence, while among those who remained and contributed to Ulster's rapid economic growth there were some who were quick to espouse the cause of revolutionary France in 1789 and to link it to the case for a radical change in Ireland's constitutional relationship to Britain. This was championed by the Society of United Irishmen formed in Belfast in October 1791. Initially supported by professional and literary men there and in Dublin, the society broadened its base within Ulster's mercantile community and moved towards the cause of a secular republic with equal rights for Catholic, Protestant and Dissenter. War between Britain and republican France made it a dangerous cause to uphold and in 1798, the year of the bloody but abortive United Irish rising, Ulster democrats like Henry Joy McCracken and many others, artisans, weavers and tenant farmers paid with their lives for supporting it.

They were never more than a minority within a Protestant community fearful of any threat to

Battle of Aughrim, 1691.

its link with the British crown. The 1790s were a tense decade in which many Protestants, especially in County Armagh and County Down, felt threatened by the mechanisation of linen weaving as well as by Catholics entering the trade. They reacted as well to the leases of vacant farms going to Catholics, also to the gradual repeal of earlier eighteenth century penal laws restricting Catholic rights. The formation of secret societies, ready to act outside the law to resist these changes, came easily to such people.

Best known amongst these were the Peep O'Day Boys, possibly formed as early as 1779 who, generally under cover of darkness, raided Catholic homes, ostensibly to seize weapons but also to commit murder. Their violence was matched and often surpassed by the Catholic Defenders, an equally secretive and ruthless body which spread out from the Ulster counties to other parts of Ireland and made some links with the United Irish movement.

It was once believed that the Peep O'Day boys founded the Orange Order in Armagh in 1795 but it is more likely that the driving force behind its emergence was Protestants who had

King William III of Orange.

acquired military training in the Volunteer regiments raised to resist a French invasion of Ireland, which was feared during the later phase of Britain's war with the rebel American colonies.

The first Orange Lodges were founded in and near Loughall in Armagh. This attractive village was the scene in 1987 of an operation by British undercover forces which wiped out an entire eight man IRA unit. In 1795 the area had seen vicious encounters between Peep O'Day Boys and Defenders and there were still vivid memories of a Protestant schoolmaster whose tongue and fingers had been cut off, four years earlier, along with those of a thirteen year old boy related to him.

The formation of Orange Lodges was an attempt by local landowners and gentry to keep control of Protestant violence and to give, through a network of local lodges, a respectable face to loyalty to the crown. This loyalty could be uncompromisingly stated, as the following Orange toast dating back to this period makes clear.

'To the glorious, pious and immortal memory of King William III, the Prince of Orange, who saved us from rogues and roguery, slaves and slavery, knaves and knavery, from Popes and Popery, from brass money and wooden shoes; and whosoever denies this toast, let him be slammed, crammed and jammed into the muzzle of the great gun of Athlone and the gun fired into the Pope's belly and the Pope fired into Hell and the door of Hell locked and the key placed in a loyal Orangeman's pocket.'

The rapid growth of Orangeism fed Catholic fears of its links to reprisals being mounted against them in a turbulent period. These fears had some justification as in the conflict that broke out after 1969, but many Orangemen in the 1790s preferred to enlist in the legitimate forces of the crown, yeomanry and militia units which helped crush the 1798 United Irish rebellion. This outcome was closely followed by the 1801 legislative union between Ireland and Britain.

Orangemen responded ambivalently to this, fearing concessions to Catholics with which London politicians might seek to sweeten the deal. These took time to materialise and for Irish Protestants and those in Ulster in particular the 1801 Act of Union became central to what they saw as an integral relationship with the Protestant British Crown.

Maintenance of or repeal of the Union came to define the politics of the Irish question for the next century. As predominantly Catholic political nationalism found its voice and achieved effective representation at Westminster under great leaders like Daniel O'Connell and Charles Parnell, Protestant Ulster came to see itself as occupying the front

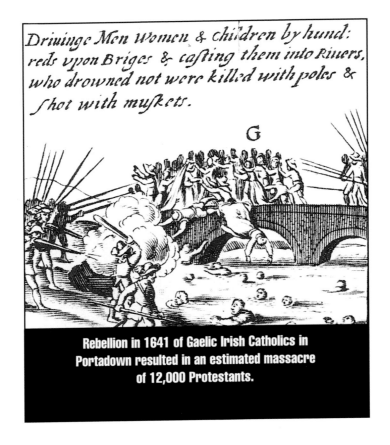

Driuinge Men women & children by hund: reds vpon Briges & cafting them into Riuers, who drowned not were killed with poles & fhot with mufkets.

Rebellion in 1641 of Gaelic Irish Catholics in Portadown resulted in an estimated massacre of 12,000 Protestants.

line of the Union's defence. The tradition of making a reality of this defence by violent and unlawful action remained and in some ways grew stronger.

It could manifest itself in the determination of Orangemen to parade even at times and through areas forbidden by the law. After a bloody encounter between them and Catholics at Dolly's Brae in County Down in 1849, an episode celebrated to this day in tunes played by Ulster's marching flute bands, a Party Processions Act was passed to outlaw provocative parades. William Johnston of Ballykilbeg became a popular hero for going to

prison over his defiance of this ban and the legislation was abandoned as unworkable in 1872.

Much violence attended this controversy, as it did attempts by Liberal governments in London to enact Home Rule bills. The Belfast Home Rule riots of 1886 cost dozens of lives and troops had to be brought in to help the police keep control. That crisis, and a second one over Gladstone's next attempt at Home Rule when he returned to office in 1892, set the scene for the much greater drama of 1912 when an Ulster Protestant vigilante and paramilitary tradition would move to centre stage.

Loyalist postcard from the early 20th-century. Bonar Law, the Conservative opposition leader is represented as a policeman, using a symbolic Red Hand of Ulster to block Irish Home Rule. This aspiration to Home Rule is portrayed by Asquith, the Liberal Prime Minister during the 1912-14 crisis, driving a donkey cart.

ACE ♣

Mr. BONAR LAW

CAPT. J. CRAIG

ACE ♠

COL. WALLACE

THE
RED HAND
AND THE
WINNING
HAND.

ULSTER

Home Rule may
Pass Parliament but.
Belfast Never—

NO SURRENDER

SIR. E. CARSON, K.C.M.P

No Home Rule

UNITED WE STAND

DIVIDED WE FALL

PAT   JOHN BULL   SANDY   TAFFY

JOHN CLELAND & SON, L?P BELFAST   IRELAND.   ENGLAND.   SCOTLAND.   WALES.

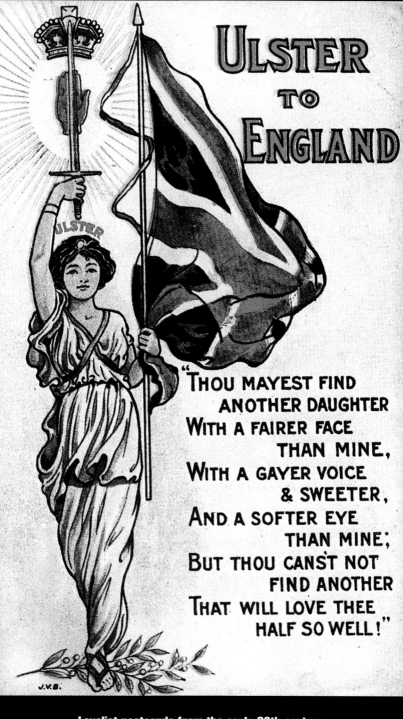

ULSTER
TO
ENGLAND

"THOU MAYEST FIND
ANOTHER DAUGHTER
WITH A FAIRER FACE
THAN MINE,
WITH A GAYER VOICE
& SWEETER,
AND A SOFTER EYE
THAN MINE;
BUT THOU CANST NOT
FIND ANOTHER
THAT WILL LOVE THEE
HALF SO WELL!"

Loyalist postcards from the early 20th-century.

CHAPTER TWO

CARSON'S ARMY, PARTITION AND THE DEFENCE OF NORTHERN IRELAND

By 1912 the prospect of Home Rule loomed dramatically larger in the collective mind of Protestant Ulster because a Liberal government in London had removed the veto power over legislation traditionally exercised by the House of Lords. This, along with the increasingly militant and confident posture of an Irish Catholic church closely linked to the country's constitutional nationalist party, deepened Ulster's existing religious and ethnic divisions.

Even previously Liberal Presbyterians began to identify themselves uncritically with the Unionist cause, seeing the Home Rule movement, in the words of Dr Conor Cruise O'Brien, as one which held to the view 'that they had a right to secede from the United Kingdom but that Unionists did not have the right to secede from the entity they sought to create'.

Home Rule was at least the policy of nationalist leaders like John Redmond who were constitutionalists. Much more radical voices could be heard from within Sinn Fein, founded by Arthur Griffith and others in 1905, and its still small membership overlapped with that of the conspiratorial and violent Irish Republican Brotherhood, or Fenians, precursors of what became the IRA and the architects of the 1916 rising.

Unionist Ireland as a whole closed ranks but it was in Ulster, with its industry and trade tied closely to British markets and investment, that opposition was fiercest. An Ulster Unionist Council had been formed in Belfast in 1905 to mobilise a growing Protestant electorate and by 1912 it had already created the basis of a formidable alliance between 'big house' leaders from the aristocracy, gentry and business and shipyard workers, artisans and tenant farmers.

Among these leaders were James Craig, later the first Prime Minister of Northern Ireland, and Frederick Crawford, both ex-soldiers and survivors of the Boer War. They however were happy to accept the leadership of Unionism at Westminster of Sir Edward Carson, a Dublin-based barrister and charismatic orator. More so than Craig, as future events would show, he was an implacable opponent of any form of Home Rule who believed that Ulster was simply the weapon with which to block it.

His magnetism on the platform complemented Craig's organisational skills. Huge shows of Unionist strength at open-air rallies culminated on 28 September 1912 with the declaration at Belfast City Hall of the Ulster Covenant. Over 470,000 Protestants signed it, pledging themselves to 'stand by one another in defending for ourselves and our children our cherished position of equal citizenship in the United Kingdom and in using all means which may be found necessary to defeat the present conspiracy to set up a Home Rule Parliament in Ireland.'

This was the language of defiance and it was already being backed up by drilling and parades on the estates of Ulster's great titled families, by those who supported the Covenant. In January 1913, the Ulster Unionist Council announced the formation of the Ulster Volunteer Force. Organised and led in the main by former army officers of varying ability and ages, it rapidly built up its active strength to nearly 100,000 men.

Its emergence is still celebrated on countless Loyalist murals in Belfast and elsewhere. These are often in areas dominated by today's UVF, a far smaller, secretive and elitist Loyalist paramilitary group which emerged in the mid 1960s and played an important and often bloody role in the conflict which resurfaced in Northern Ireland at the end of that decade.

Whether 'Carson's army' really had the will or the resources with which to thwart the will of an elected government and take on its armed forces was never put to the test. War in Europe in August 1914 averted that but the matter has been widely debated by historians. Some have argued that the UVF's unit structure of regiments and battalions, influenced largely by the British army model, concealed wide variations in its manpower and competence levels. These could differ from area to area as could attendance at drills. In March 1914, the Inspector-General of the Royal Irish Constabulary believed that only one-third of the UVF's members were ready for real military action.

At that stage, many of them still had no experience of handling real weapons. The celebrated gun-running operation in April 1914, as a result of which twenty five thousand German rifles and three million rounds of ammunition were landed at the port of Larne and safely distributed to UVF units, was a huge morale-booster yet it still left them without artillery and with very few machine guns. The UVF might well have been able to defeat the nationalist Irish Volunteers, formed in response to its own emergence, or the RIC, but against regular British troops its best course of action would have been localised guerrilla tactics.

The first drill of Ulstermen 5 June 1912.

Craig and Carson knew well the political hazards of Ulstermen proving their loyalty by attacking British forces and may, by the summer of 1914, have come to think of the UVF as merely providing useful muscle for Unionism with its parades and shows of strength. While its discipline could vary its membership did not get drawn into indiscriminate sectarian attacks on the nationalist community. To leaders who remembered the carnage of the Belfast Home Rule riots less than thirty years earlier that was an important consideration.

When Britain declared war on Germany on 4 August 1914, Craig and Carson accepted that a much greater peril to both the union and the crown had arisen. There had been inconclusive talk prior to then about partition in the form of a temporary exclusion of at least some Ulster counties from Home Rule. Carson had dismissed this as a mere 'stay of execution'. Once war had begun, however, he declined to press for any amending bill to the Home Rule legislation which had become law.

Instead there was all-party agreement at Westminster to suspend Home Rule either for twelve months or until the war ended. It was then that the UVF's role became in a real sense a military one as many of its members enlisted in Lord Kitchener's 'New Army'. Not all did. Especially in Belfast, distrust of British intentions made some hold back from volunteering and over the four years of conflict

Ulster Protestants in the crown forces were outnumbered by Catholics from their own counties and the rest of Ireland. For them, serving Britain in its hour of need and in a war for the rights of small nations would, they believed, bring Home Rule as their reward.

Claims that UVF men who were also Orangemen wore their collarettes and sashes and yelled 'no surrender' as they climbed out of their trenches on the Somme on 1 July, 1916 may be the stuff of legend but the sacrifice made on that day and in later actions by the 36th Ulster Division is a matter of record. Thousands of white headstones are testimony to it in the military cemeteries near Thiepval and the site of the formidable Schwaben Redoubt which the Ulstermen stormed at terrible cost.

Loyal Ulster mourned but also felt it had now paid in blood any debts it owed to Britain. The slaughter on the Somme moreover followed hard upon events in Dublin, where the Easter 1916 rebellion seemed to represent proof of the treachery which lurked within nationalist Ireland. The Irish Republican Brotherhood which had planned the rising had support in the North, particularly in Belfast, while in the December 1918 General Election Sinn Fein made gains in Ulster as it did in Ireland as a whole, virtually eliminating Redmond's Nationalist party from the electoral map.

ULSTER 1914.

DESERTED!
WELL—I CAN STAND ALONE.

Loyalist postcard.

Irish First World War recruiting poster. Both Catholic and Protestant
volunteered to fight in the British army from across Ireland.

Michael Collins, left, the IRA leader and Commmander-in-Chief of the new Irish Free State army with General Richard Mulcahy, who replaced him after his assasination by anti-treaty IRA members.

The 36th Ulster Division, formed from the original UVF, at the battle of the Somme.

Sir James Craig, first Prime Minster of Northern Ireland.

As tensions mounted and the IRA resorted to all-out war against a British presence in Ireland, the basis for any self-governing all-Irish state, if it had ever existed, began to crumble away. A partitionist settlement, involving power devolved from London to a six-county mini-state in Northern Ireland became the best fallback position for Ulster Unionists, though Carson only accepted it with bitter reluctance.

He was no bigot, however. There were Irish language speakers in his family and he had played hurling when young. He was quick to warn of the dangers of any northern state which excluded or victimised Catholics but he had little real influence over the events which accompanied and followed partition in 1920.

Northern Ireland's devolved administration and Parliament were brought to birth amidst a bloodbath of communal violence. An ongoing IRA campaign, which often took innocent lives, was paralleled by a wave of attacks on the new state's nationalist minority. In April 1920, men who had been in the UVF took control of the centre of Londonderry and used the city's walls to direct fire into the Catholic Bogside area below them. The IRA counter-attacked and two months of fighting there took forty lives despite the imposition of a curfew by the army.

The UVF was not the centrally-led force which it had been in 1914, though some attempt was made to revive it in rural areas such as Fermanagh. In Belfast, the epicentre of sectarian killing in this period, former members often took the law into their own hands either in response to IRA attacks or simply to terrorise nationalist areas of the city believing, like their successors half a century later, that they were simply fighting fire with fire even if it was often the innocent who were victims. In June 1920, leading Ulster Unionists gave their support to reactivating the UVF throughout the six counties which would soon become the new devolved entity of Northern Ireland. Tension mounted as the legislation to bring this into being went through the Westminster Parliament. While the Loyalist marching season got under way, Catholic workers were driven from their work in Belfast's shipyards and engineering works. They were an easily targeted minority and were helped on their way by 'Belfast confetti', lethal volleys of iron bolts and rivets. At the height of the 'Twelfth Week', twenty lives were lost and Sir James Craig, soon to become Prime Minister of Northern Ireland, spoke of imminent civil war and the case for 'organised reprisals'.

A new Ulster Special Constabulary was formed, divided into an A category full time force of 2,000 men and B and C special reserves. All were armed and many UVF men joined as the killing intensified, fuelling Catholic and nationalist fears of their community's vulnerability to attack. From July 1920 to July 1922, four hundred and fifty three people were killed in Belfast,two hundred and fifty seven of them Catholics, one hundred and fifty seven Protestants and two of unstated religious allegiance. Thirty seven members of the security force also lost their lives, almost all by IRA attacks.

One man widely suspected of an active role in this awful spasm of hate-filled violence was police District Inspector John Nixon. His name was linked to what happened in the early hours of the morning of 24 March, 1922 in a house which is still occupied, at 3 Kinnaird Terrace, just off the Antrim Road. Owen McMahon, a popular Catholic publican, five of his sons and an employee lodging with the family, were roused by armed intruders who gave them a few moments for prayer before cutting them down in a hail of revolver fire.

Only two of them survived and the funerals of the others became a huge event, thousands of people lining the route to Milltown cemetery four days later and packing the burial area. Two B-Special officers had been shot dead near the McMahon home the previous day so the massacre was widely seen in nationalist Belfast as a police reprisal. This has never been proved conclusively. If it was, it may well have involved 'Specials' who were also in the UVF or the Ulster Protestant Association, another vigilante group formed at this time.

It came at a moment when Michael Collins, a leading Minister in the new Irish Free State and Sir James Craig had in fact reached an agreement under which, in return for an end to IRA attacks in Northern Ireland, inducements would be made available to Catholics to join the Special Constabulary and those intimidated out of work would be given back their jobs.

The following month saw the formation of the Royal Ulster Constabulary. It recruited almost 50,000 full and part-time officers, almost all Protestant, armed not merely with their own weapons but with the formidable authority given them by the province's Special Powers Act. These developments led to the effective disbandment of the UVF as the new force began to assert itself. The horror of the years from 1920 to 1922 left deep scars but sectarian killing was brought under control and in February 1924, Inspector Nixon, prime suspect in the murder of the McMahons was suspended by the RUC, not because of this but for an inflammatory speech he had made in an Orange Hall.

It did not prevent Nixon making a career for himself in Unionist and later Independent Unionist politics. He was also suspected of being close to a revived Ulster Protestant Association, armed members of which were believed to be involved in the serious sectarian violence of the summer of 1935. This was brought on by the bitterness which came with mounting unemployment but what set it off was rifle-fire directed at an Orange walk in North Belfast as the twelfth anniversary parades drew near.

Sustained communal violence followed, bringing British troops on to the streets in support of the RUC. Property was set on fire, families evicted from their homes in what would later be called 'inter-face' areas and thirteen people were killed. Some Ulster Protestant Association gunmen were involved and their identities were known within their own community. One was a legendary character known as 'Buck Alex' who lived on the city's York Road and is said to have kept a lion in his backyard. Even in the 1960s, Catholic mothers in Belfast are known to have used his name and ferocious reputation to scare small children who were misbehaving.

The Second World War brought economic recovery and relatively high employment back to much of Northern Ireland. It brought too a Labour government in London whose welfare legislation covered the province but the tensions endemic to a still-divided community remained. They moved closer to the surface in 1949, when the Irish state broke its last links with Britain and proclaimed itself a republic and when, in December 1956, the IRA, regrouped after the setbacks and divisions that arose from its ill-fated January 1939 'declaration of war' against Britain, embarked upon its border campaign against Northern Ireland and the 'British presence' it was thought to represent.

Even before this futile and murderous enterprise, some Ulster Protestants had sensed danger and met in Belfast to form Ulster Protestant Action. The first year of its existence was much taken up with the discussion of vigilante patrols, street barricades and compiling lists of IRA suspects both in Belfast and rural areas. Factory and workplace branches were set up and the new organisation remained in being even when it became clear that IRA operations were being limited to the border.

Among those involved were Unionists and Loyalists who would become major politcal figures in the 1960s and 1970s. One of them was the young fundamentalist preacher Ian Paisley. For him, and many others, the real danger was starting to seem not just the IRA but an experiment in a modestly liberal Unionism ready to accept at least some of the minority community's demands. In June 1959, Paisley received his first conviction for a public order offence after attacks on Catholic homes had followed a speech he had made to a Shankill Road audience.

Four years later, Terence O'Neill's appointment as Prime Minister and his apparent commitment to a reformist agenda and creating a more benign image for Northern Ireland would bring Paisley and his supporters into the limelight. It would also bring back into being the Ulster Volunteer Force.

GOD, GUNS AND ULSTER

Murals from Usiter.
Most of the imagery from the lower left mural has
religious assocations.

The Rev. Robert Bradford was the Unionist MP for South Belfast
murdered by the IRA in November 1981.

CHAPTER THREE

THE ULSTER VOLUNTEER FORCE

Augustus Spence, or 'Gusty' Spence, as he has always been known, a Protestant shipyard worker who had served in the Royal Ulster Rifles and was active in his local Orange Lodge, accepted a lift early in 1965 to a farm near the village of Pomeroy in County Tyrone. Once there, he recalls, he and three other men who had travelled with him were shown into a building like a farm, lit by hurricane lamps. In the presence of around forty people, he was sworn into membership of the Ulster Volunteer Force. The man who presided over the ceremony, he has also recalled, was a former British army colonel.

Tensions were already on the increase in Northern Ireland. Captain O'Neill, the Unionist Prime Minister, was pressing ahead with initiatives conciliatory to the Catholic community but distrusted deeply by many Unionists and Orangemen. The IRA's border campaign had been abandoned but both the republican movement and the Irish government in Dublin had ambitious plans for the celebration of the fiftieth anniversary the

following year of the 1916 Easter rebellion. The IRA's Dublin-based leadership had in fact virtually abandoned armed struggle and was looking for a political strategy to replace it but Spence and others like him knew little of this. They were part of a process by which a new UVF, proud of its historic antecedents, began to recruit and organise.

Spence rose to a position of command in the Shankill unit of the UVF which early in 1966 carried out fire bombings, one of them against the Holy Cross Girls' School in Ardoyne, where Captain O'Neill was due to address a conference on ways of promoting goodwill between Protestant and Catholic communities. Nearly forty years later, an often violent Loyalist picket of the school would make it world-famous.

In May, however, the UVF began to kill. Their first and unintended victim was a Protestant, seventy seven year old Mrs Matilda Gould whose house in the Shankill area was mistaken by them for that of a Catholic who lived next

A British soldier on patrol on the Shankill Road.

Gusty Spence, centre, in an Ulster Volunteer Force colour party, Compound 21, Long Kesh, 1976.

door. She died of her burns seven weeks later. By then the UVF had murdered two young Catholics in the same part of Belfast.

The RUC, knowing who they were looking for, acted promptly, arresting Spence and two other men. In October after the longest trial in Northern Ireland's history, they received minimum sentences of twenty years each for the murder of one of their victims, an eighteen year old Catholic barman, Peter Ward. The trial yielded evidence of heavy drinking before the killing, the acquisition and concealment of illegal weapons, and also the claim by one of Spence's co-accused that he had joined the UVF under the influence of Ian Paisley.

This could never have been proved and Paisley's newspaper, the Protestant Telegraph was quick to condemn the murders. It is as likely that encouragement to men like Gusty Spence came from dissident elements within the Ulster Unionist Party, though he has never been prepared to name them. Well ahead of his trial, the government of Northern Ireland declared the UVF an illegal organisation but it retained much of its structure and continued to recruit members despite RUC surveillance. It did this while the political situation deteriorated rapidly as marches by the new Northern Ireland Civil Rights Association backed by left wing Queen's University student groups, challenged traditional Unionist control of the streets.

Further UVF bomb attacks, some of them planned in such a way as to be blamed on the IRA, helped to further destabilise the community and when Captain O'Neill resigned as Prime Minister on 28 April, 1969 amidst street confrontations and growing violence, the Belfast-born poet John Hewitt captured the danger vividly in his fine poem 'Coasters', published in the same year:

> 'The cloud of infection hangs over the city,
> a quick change of wind and it
> might spill over the leafy suburbs'

By 1971, with both the new Provisional IRA and the Official movement from which it had split ready for war, not just in defence of nationalist areas but against partition itself, the UVF was also ready to take on and 'take out' the republican enemy. It was rapidly drawn into a downward spiral of ruthlessness as British troops struggled to keep control and entire localities were abandoned by their populations fleeing to the safety offered by their co-religionists.

For example, early in December 1971, in response to nakedly sectarian IRA attacks on Protestant pubs, the UVF left a powerful bomb in the entrance to McGurk's, a Catholic-owned bar on Belfast's North Queen Street. Gusty Spence has recalled hearing the resulting explosion from his cell a mile away in Crumlin Road prison. Fifteen people died in the worst atrocity carried out at that point in the troubles. Flinching from the horror of what had happened, the UVF did not admit responsibility but seven years later one of their members, while in police custody, admitted to his part in the bombing and received a life sentence. His accomplice was never identified.

A year later, UVF bombs in Dublin and in towns on the Irish border took three lives and caused many injuries, part of a strategy, it was claimed, to force the Dublin government to enact tough legislation against the IRA within its own borders. Infinitely worse carnage was unleashed on the Irish capital and on the border town of Monaghan on 17 May, 1974, when UVF units from Belfast and Armagh set off no-warning car bombs in both places during the early Friday evening rush hour. Twenty eight people were killed in Dublin, twenty of them women and two small children. There and in Monaghan many bodies were mutilated to the point where they were barely identifiable.

David Ervine, a former UVF prisoner and Loyalist politician, speaking on television twenty years after the attacks, said that they were 'returning the serve', meaning that indiscriminate IRA violence in Northern Ireland was being repaid in like kind by those who had the will to do it. There was more to the 17 May bombings than that, however: Northern Ireland was close to paralysis from a strike organised by the Ulster Workers Council to bring down a power-sharing executive set up by London but supported by the Dublin government. An ill-judged Council of Ireland was also part of the package and deeply distrusted by most Unionists.

The Dublin and Monaghan bombings were thus a calculated warning to Dublin to cease meddling in Northern Ireland's political future, though the power-sharing experiment collapsed quickly. Whether the UVF acted unaided or received help from British under-cover forces has been debated over the years. The IRA and some of its well-wishers in the media have sought to exploit this debate but Henry McDonald and Jim Cusack, in their definitive book on the UVF accepted the organisation's assertions that it attacked Dublin and Monaghan unaided.

At the time the question was raised in quarters concerned to talk down the UVF's capabilities as a paramilitary group. In fact it was still recruiting well in 1974 though never tempted to mobilise the mass membership which the Ulster Defence Association achieved in 1972 and 1973 and could openly demonstrate on street rallies and marches. The UVF's image of itself was that of a tightly disciplined secret army, probably never numbering more than 1400 active members but, like the IRA, relying on intelligence-gathering, safe houses and other forms of help from supportive elements within the Loyalist working-class community.

Gusty Spence near his former home in the Lower Shankill district.

The scene in the Pentecostal Church hall in Darkley, County Armagh, on 21 November 1983, after gunmen connected to the Irish National Liberation Army opened fire on the congregation. three people were killed and seven others were severely wounded. This attack caused particular outrage to Loyalist Ulster.

The UVF drew regular recruits from its youth wing, the Young Citizen Volunteers and in 1972 reached a working agreement with another paramilitary body whose operations were in danger of overlapping with its own. This was the Red Hand Commando, whose leaders agreed to close co-operation on all matters with the UVF while retaining their own organisational identity. Their colour parties, in distinctive black combat kit, still appear regularly at UVF band parades and commemorations.

The UVF killed 534 people during the troubles and has murdered others since the 1994 cease-fires. Its bloodiest years were in the 1970s when it took 365 lives, including those of the bombing victims already referred to in Dublin and Monaghan. To this day the UVF magazine Combat gives much space in every issue to photos and articles celebrating what it perceives as the feats of volunteers who fought to defend their Ulster and the Union against republican aggression.

A probable fifty five UVF and Red Hand Commando members were killed in the troubles by the IRA and the security forces and some in vicious feuds with the UDA which re-surfaced in the year 2000. On occasions the UVF did have major successes in taking the war directly to the enemy. In February 1981 a lone gunman, Robert 'Squeak' Seymour, travelled the short distance involved from his own home in Belfast to shoot dead as he slept Jim 'Skipper'

Burns, a particularly vicious thug who held rank in the Belfast IRA.

Ten years later, in March 1991, two UVF units from East Tyrone penetrated the fiercely republican village of Cappagh to attack the local pub where they killed three key members of the mid-Ulster IRA. Soon afterwards the UVF joined the UDA in forming the Combined Loyalist Military Command to co-ordinate operations against the IRA. Rogue elements within the UDA were reported to be a matter of concern to the UVF leadership, even after the Command's formation but both organisations took their war relentlessly closer to republican leaders.

As always the innocent continued to suffer. The UVF, for all its claims to military discipline, had never had total control over maverick and compulsively brutal elements within its ranks. A prime example was the Shankill Butchers, a Loyalist gang who terrorised West Belfast in the mid-1970s. Their leader Lennie Murphy, who had acquired a criminal record even as a teenager, chose to define the terms of his own relationship with the UVF and even Gusty Spence, with the authority he exercised over Loyalist prisoners, found him hard to control when he was serving time for illegal possession of weapons. In fact Murphy directed some of his gang's worst killings from within prison but took an eager part in others. Victims, nearly all Catholics, were usually abducted with the use of black taxis then tortured and beaten to death. Murphy is known to have used a meat-packer's knife to cut some victims' throats back to the spine

The gang were finally brought to trial in late 1978, though not all of them and not Murphy, whose prison sentence was his alibi. Eleven of them were given life sentences for a total of eighteen murders. Murphy was shot dead soon after his release in November 1982. His killing was claimed by the IRA but set up by elements within the UDA resentful of what they saw as his designs on territory in Belfast which they controlled for 'fund raising'.

Murphy's funeral was a significant Loyalist event. There were many mourners and his headstone

Ulster Volunter Force firing party beside the coffin of John Bingham, a UVF commander in north Belfast, shot dead at his home by the IRA 14 September 1986. His funeral drew a huge attendance.

in Carnmoney cemetery is carved with the insignia of the UVF and also the words 'Here lies a soldier'. Only feet away lies one of his victims, Steven McCann, a gentle 21 year old student whose body was almost decapitated when RUC officers found him in an alley off the Shankill Road in October 1976.

Driven possibly by dark urges within many of them, by heavy drinking, visceral hatred and fear of what they thought was Catholic encroachment into available housing in what had once been Loyalist areas, or indeed by a combination of all these factors, Murphy's gang dragged the conflict in Northern Ireland to its lowest depths. Memories are long in Belfast and when Bobby 'Basher' Bates, one of Murphy's lieutenants, finished his sentence in 1997, having declared himself to be a born-again Christian, he was shot dead within weeks, probably by a close relative of one of his Protestant victims.

In prison, Gusty Spence did what he could to help bring sectarian murder under control. This was an important part of a journey to personal redemption but his influence on fellow prisoners was greater within Crumlin Road and Long Kesh than it was outside. From early on in his sentence, he read and studied and encouraged others to do the same. He also listened to the views of republican prisoners, especially those of the Official IRA which called its own ceasefire in May 1972.

'Why are you here?' is a question David Ervine remembers Spence putting to him when he arrived to start his own sentence. It was Spence's attempt to make young Loyalists think about whether the acts which earned them imprisonment had rational political goals. As early as 1973, some UVF members in Belfast 'went political', forming the Volunteer Protestant Party to contest elections on class issues instead of just the old appeals to Loyalist solidarity. This seemed to make sense for an organisation whose support base was solidly working class but politically the UVF lacked cohesion. As within the UDA a young skinhead element was attracted to the British National Front and they were apathetic or hostile to the new party which achieved only limited electoral success. In response to a ceasefire announced by the UVF in November 1973, the ban on it was lifted in April of the following year by Merlyn Rees, the Secretary of State for Northern Ireland.

Deep divisions within the UVF resulted from these developments and after a savage sequence of killings carried out over several months, it was once more proscribed in October 1975. The many arrests by the security forces which followed the re-imposition of the ban did little to reduce their capacity to kill, which increased the next year. In desperation the authorities allowed Catholic and Protestant clergy to hold talks with Gusty Spence in Long Kesh about how the

slaughter outside the prison might be brought under control.

This was easier to call for than to achieve. The UVF's reply was that it would support initiatives to halt the killing but only in the larger context of a 'complete cessation of all violence' which it defined as meaning an end to IRA attacks on the security forces as well as property and commercial targets. Exhausted and frustrated, in September of 1976 Spence resigned his position as Commanding Officer of the UVF and Red Hand Commando prisoners but his personal and political influence continued to be important to many of them. Without it, men like Ervine and Billy Hutchison would not have played, along with Gusty Spence himself, the part they did in what became the 'peace process' of the 1990s.

What did develop from the sort of debates which Spence had encouraged was the emergence of the Progressive Unionist Party. In 1977 it brought out a policy document making the case for a new experiment in power-sharing between Northern Ireland's two communities, but one which would be negotiated and not imposed. The UDA began also to feel its way in this direction although, in contrast to the fundamentally Unionist UVF, it associated itself for a time with the idea of full independence for Ulster.

The road to any sort of peace was a long one and UVF volunteers continued to kill, sometimes ruthlessly and at random, right into the summer of 1994. On 18 June of that year, a UVF unit entered the only pub in Loughinisland, a village in County Down, and used automatic weapons to blast local people watching Ireland's opening World Cup game. Six people were killed, including an eighty-seven year old grandfather, and five wounded. None had any known republican connections.

Soon afterwards, two Belfast journalists were told by the UVF in Belfast that the killers had acted without authorisation, though what they did was almost certainly their revenge for the shooting of three UVF men on the Shankill Road two days before. Further killings were carried out by the UVF even as its political

The November 1985 Hillsborough agreement signed by Margaret Thatcher and the Irish Taoiseach, Garret Fitzgerald, upheld the principle of majority consent to the union in Northern Ireland, but it allowed Dublin to be consulted on major areas of British rule there. Unionist leaders like Dr Paisley and James Molyneaux led huge protest rallies.

Bomb attack by the IRA on the Europa Hotel.

years of the troubles, the bodies of Loyalist paramilitary victims were sometimes dumped by their killers.

Gusty Spence, who had done much good work for reconciliation in Northern Ireland since his release from prison ten years earlier, read out the Loyalist statement. It paid tribute 'to all our Fighters, Commandos and Volunteers who have paid the supreme sacrifice. They did not die in vain. The union is safe.' In a later passage the statement declared: 'In all sincerity, we offer to the loved ones of all innocent victims over the past twenty five years abject and true remorse. No amount of our words will compensate for the intolerable suffering they have undergone during the conflict.'

These were words and sentiments absent from the 31 August communiqué in which the IRA had announced an end to its savage, sectarian and divisive attempt to bring about an imposed unification of Ireland. Their guns and bombs had claimed twice as many lives as those of the Loyalists. Northern Ireland however, had still not seen the last killings by the Ulster Volunteer Force or by the Ulster Defence Association.

An appearence of members of the IRA in the Ardoyne area of north Belfast before calling their July 1997 ceasefire.

A display of pipe bombs. These weapons were used by Ulster Freedom Fighters in attacks on Nationalist people's home, especially at 'interface' areas of Belfast and also in towns like Larne over a four year period after the 1988 Belfast agreement.

David Ervine, of the Progressive Unionist Party, 15 August 1997

Street mural off Shankhill Road. The Red Hand Commando has carried out killings on behalf of the UVF over many years.

Colour party in black combat kit are Red Hand Commando members.

UVF band Parade, July 1999 to mark the killing on 9 July 1999 of Trevor King, a senoir UVF member, ranking as Brigadier. He was shot dead on the Shankhill Road by INLA gunmen.

Mural in Woodvale. A volley fired in honour of Brian Robinson, a member of the UVF, killed by special forces in 1988.

Members of the Apprentice Boys of Derry parading at their church inside inside Derry's walls, 10 August 1996.

Ulster parade. The satirical placard shows Sinn Fein member Gerry Kelly as an Orangeman during a 12th of July parade on the Crumlin Road.

remained local, a response to danger identified at street level, but a structure of command began to emerge as ever increasing numbers of mainly young Loyalists began to join. In late January of 1972, a large number of vigilante and defence groups like Fogel's came together to form the Ulster Defence Association. Its first chairman and commandant was Charles Harding-Smith, a tyre salesman and former shipyard worker who lived only a couple of streets away from David Fogel.

In Woodvale, Fogel took overall command. He had no special hatred for Catholics whose living conditions in nearby nationalist areas were, he realised, little different from his own, but he blamed them for identifying themselves with a republican movement whose ambitions were a threat to everything he and his neighbours believed in. Politics were part of the agenda too in these early days.

'We felt let down by the Unionists,' Fogel told an interviewer in 1973. 'We didn't want these middle-class smarty pants ponceing down our streets once every five years asking for our votes and then never bothering to come again until the next election.' Moving on from simple rejection of old Unionism to a political programme with real appeal for working-class Loyalists was an urgent necessity but one which could easily be crowded out by day-to-day developments.

1972 was a year of trauma for Northern Ireland, marked out by Bloody Sunday, the imposition of direct government by Britain and intensified and indiscriminate gun and bomb attacks by an IRA growing in confidence. It was also a year in which the UDA became a real force to reckon with. In answer to what the IRA was already doing in much of Belfast and Londonderry, the UDA in Woodvale decided in late May to build street barricades in order to create its own 'no-go area'.

They did this successfully over a twenty four hour period, with full media coverage and without the security forces acting to stop them. The result was a major boost to UDA morale. Within days of this happening, Fogel and Harding-Smith were at Stormont putting their views to William Whitelaw, the recently-appointed Secretary of State and later in June 1972 the UDA marched through central Belfast, thousands strong and clad in combat kit, dark eyeshades, forage caps and bush hats.

By this time they had started to kill, or some of them had, victims being selected very much on the basis of local decisions made with minimal reference to a still evolving command structure and often in response to specific actions by the IRA. Increasingly however, as the situation worsened, it became, on the admission of those involved at the time, a case of 'any Taig will do' but 'disloyal Protestants' suspected of having

UDA murals in Belfast's Shankill area.

Anti-Catholic slogans in Larne, County Antrim, 20 March 1998

UDA memebers march through Belfast streets, 1973.

UDA funeral, 1972.

Catholic friends or drinking in the 'wrong' pubs and clubs, became part of the mounting body count.

The truly awful ferocity of many of these killings grew out of a frenzy of Loyalist fear and rage at IRA bombs which tore apart and mutilated the innocent, some of them small children, in soft targets like restaurants, shops and bus stations. This can never excuse, though it helps to explain the way a growing number of UDA murders were preceded by the protracted torture of victims in 'romper rooms', macabrely named after a then popular children's television programme.

One of the most appalling episodes of this period was the double murder by a UDA member in June 1973 of a former member of the Stormont Senate, the Catholic Paddy Wilson, and a Protestant friend, Irene Andrews. Five year later, John White, who would after his eventual release from prison become a political spokesman for the UDA, was convicted of both killings, in which a large knife had inflicted dozens of wounds on the victims before they died. White expressed regret at killing a Protestant in error but told the court 'any Roman Catholic would have done. A lot of Protestants had been killed by the IRA at that time. I could see the IRA taking over Ulster and I was against this. I thought if I killed Roman Catholics it would stop them.'

Responsibility for an increasing number of UDA killings began to be claimed by the Ulster Freedom Fighters, as it would continue to do for the next twenty years. They in fact were never a separate organisation, though they seemed to be defined as such by the authorities when they were declared illegal in 1973 while the UDA was allowed to remain legal until the summer of 1992.

British Cabinet papers for 1972 now made public, suggest that some advisers to the government were of the opinion that it was a worthwhile risk to let a legal UDA serve as an outlet for Protestant frustrations and fears, and also to let UDA men, under certain conditions, enlist in the newly-formed Ulster Defence Regiment. As arrests and internment began to hit the Loyalist community, convicted UFF prisoners, almost without exception, opted to serve their sentences in UDA prison blocks and compounds.

Apart from mass membership in its early days, another way in which the UDA differed from the UVF was that some of its leaders were ready to talk openly to the media and also to get drawn into brutal power struggles. Often these were between rival brigade areas, vying with each other for control of territory and members as well as for weapons and significant funds raised by contributions, not always voluntarily made in the case of pub and shop owners.

UFF firing party after UDA/UFF march Lower Shankill, Belfast, 20 August 2000. the violence unleashed by this march launched a feud between the UDA and the UVf which took several lives.

In late 1972 and the following year, Charles Harding-Smith created deep divisions by seeming to use his Shankill power base to attempt a takeover of the whole organisation. This led to David Fogel's departure from Belfast, the murder of his second-in-command, Ernie Elliott and also that of Tommy Herron, the East Belfast brigadier, in September 1973. Harding-Smith's bid for overall power failed and this cleared the way for the rise of Andy Tyrie, who remained chairman and commandant of the Association until another power struggle forced him out in 1988.

Tyrie's long survival was an extraordinary feat. It owed much to his position in 1973 as a compromise candidate for the leadership who did not have too many real enemies within the UDA. He has also said his preference for keeping away from pubs and clubs gave such critics as he had little scope for character assassination and there was never any suspicion that he lived lavishly off the organisation's funds.

He was a former Territorial Army soldier who had been employed in the Rolls Royce engineering works and also as a landscape gardener. Some found him a forbidding figure with the tinted glasses he sometimes wore and his Zapata-style moustache, but he saw the need to let the media hear the UDA's political case. He was always accessible for tea and talk at the headquarters building on Belfast's

Newtonards Road and he encouraged younger members to take an interest in politics, such as John McMichael from Lisburn, whom he promoted to be South Belfast brigadier and his own second-in-command.

Andy Tyrie took over amidst renewed political crisis and threw the UDA's strength behind the Loyalist Association of Workers and its demonstrations and protest strikes against IRA atrocities and in favour of tougher security measures to halt them. He also supported the Vanguard movement, a militant campaign launched in 1972 against the British government's imposition of direct rule in Northern Ireland. It was led by a former Stormont Home Affairs Minister, William Craig, and became a political party in its own right in 1973, supported by, among many others, a young Queen's University law lecturer, David Trimble.

Out of the Loyalist Association of Workers and Vanguard developed the Ulster Workers Council which, initially in some secrecy, was formed in 1973 to oppose a new departure in policy under the government of Edward Heath, which called for a power-sharing executive to represent both communities and an all-Ireland Council to deliberate on issues of cross-border concern. The UWC echoed deeply-felt Protestant belief that this was an imposed package which carried with it a threat to the Union itself.

Long Kesh prison, re-named The Maze. Often called the 'IRA University', it also housed hundreds of Loyalist prisoners. Before the H-blocks were built, they took part in protests over conditions. After 1981 they got the benefits of concessions made as a result of the IRA's hunger strikes.

UDA members parading in the the Lower Shankill housing estate

The UDA on patrol in a Loyalist area in Belfast, 1973.

Two men lie awaiting medical attention after the attempted murder of Gerry Adams, 1984. One of them is John Gregg who later became UDA brigadier in South east Antrim and was shot dead on 1 February 2003.

It co-ordinated a dramatically successful strike over a two-week period in May, 1974. This brought Northern Ireland close to paralysis with Loyalist workers and the UDA in particular, taking virtual control over the distribution of many essential goods and services. Much of the Unionist population backed the protest but road blocks and forbidding pickets gave a cutting edge to a challenge which a Labour Secretary of State, Merlyn Rees, chose not to take on, certainly not if it meant using the army. The resignation of the Unionist Prime Minister of the ill-fated executive, Brian Faulkner, on 27 May, brought a huge outbreak of joy in working class Loyalist areas where there had been little to celebrate over the previous five years. There was indeed some justification for Tyrie's later claim that the UDA had been the 'brains and muscle' that had brought victory to the strikers.

It was a victory which however would not be repeated, though a half-hearted attempt to do so, much influenced by the always restless ambition of Ian Paisley, came three years later, ostensibly in protest against the failure of British measures against the IRA. Andy Tyrie admitted later to regret at the UDA's involvement in this failed venture which the security forces confronted with much more determination than in 1974.

Much bigger protests and strike action were supported by the UDA over the winter and spring of 1985-86 in response to Margaret Thatcher's determination to enforce the Anglo-Irish Agreement which gave Dublin a role in the administration of the North, especially in security matters. By then however the UDA, and working class Loyalism more generally, had lost the political initiative which the victory in 1974 seemed to have secured.

Debate about Northern Ireland's constitutional future was once again dominated by the existing Unionist parties but political thinking within an element of the UDA was stimulated by the surge of confidence which came with the triumphant outcome of the strike. With the encouragement of Andy Tyrie and also Glen Barr, a trade unionist and key figure during the strike, the New Ulster Political Research Group was formed to consider alternatives to either a return to the Stormont system or full integration with Britain, which for a period in the 1970s was supported by Ian Paisley and his Party.

In 1979, the group published 'Beyond the Religious Divide', which called for a fully independent six county Ulster state within the British Commonwealth but guaranteeing equal rights to both communities. As John McMichael put it: 'We will have to sacrifice our member-ship of the UK at some time in the future but not to accept a united Ireland.' These proposals were given serious attention by some commentators and in 1981 the UDA backed the formation of an Ulster Loyalist Democratic Party. Its chance came quickly when the sitting Westminster Unionist MP for South Belfast was murdered in November of that year by the IRA.

McMichael stood for the new party in the by-election but was bitterly disappointed by a derisory vote for it. Established patterns of class deference in Protestant voting had clearly worked against a new party with new ideas but also with working class paramilitary associations. With Andy Tyrie's backing, political discussion continued and was echoed in UDA publications like 'Ulster' and later the 'New Ulster Defender'. In 1987 a policy document called 'Common Sense' was produced, similar in content to its predecessor although it opted for devolved Ulster government within the United Kingdom.

Many political groups and individuals outside the UDA were consulted during the preparation of 'Common Sense' and it also received some very favourable media coverage. McMichael identified himself enthusiastically with this new document and argued the case for it impressively at meetings and press conferences. He remained, however, actively involved in the UDA's campaign to kill known republicans and more generally to take its war to the nationalist community.

In 1984, UDA gunmen just missed killing Sinn Fein president Gerry Adams and the level of

killing by it increased sharply after the November 1985 Anglo-Irish Agreement. Steps were taken by both McMichael and Tyrie to recruit within the UDA's ranks a specially-trained Ulster Defence Force which would be ready for full-scale operations in response to any joint sovereignty with Dublin, a possibility thought to be a real outcome of British policy at this time.

McMichael was murdered at his own home in Lisburn just before Christmas 1987. The IRA carried out the killing but he was probably the victim of another power struggle within the organisation. The next year saw Andy Tyrie forced out of power against a background of intensified killing by the UDA, exemplified when Michael Stone launched a single-handed gun and grenade attack, in Belfast's Milltown cemetery, on mourners at the burial of three IRA members killed in Gibraltar by the SAS. Gerry Adams and Martin McGuinness who were present were Stone's prime targets. There is conflicting evidence of his relationship with the UDA before this but after his arrest and conviction Stone was given a hero's welcome by its prisoners in the Maze, formerly Long Kesh, and served out his sentence in the UDA block.

After Tyrie's departure, the UDA claimed to be operating with a more collective leadership. Press briefings were given at a round table instead of the long rectangular one from which Tyrie had liked to talk and take questions. This

The scene in Belfast's Milltown Cemetery on 16 March 1988 immediately after Michael Stone's gun and grenade attack on the mourners at the funeral of three IRA volunteers killed in Gibraltar by the SAS. three people were killed in the attack and sixty-eight wounded.

Michael Stone leaving the Maze Prison for Christmas parole, 23 December 1998.

leadership was in fact infiltrated by the RUC's Special Branch, while at least one British army 'mole' was gathering 'operational' intelligence for the UDA while feeding much of it back to his controllers.

In the summer of 1991, the UDA's Inner Council joined forces with the Ulster Volunteer Force and the Red Hand Commando in a Combined Loyalist Military Command, as described in the previous chapter of this book. It was at this point that Johnny Adair came on to the Inner Council as his 'C' Company of the Lower Shankill Ulster Freedom Fighters terrorised nationalist Belfast with the ferocity of its attacks. Adair, despite his nickname 'Mad Dog' was not the main killer. This was Stephen McKeague who later died of a drug overdose, but in 1995 Adair was given a heavy prison sentence on the novel charge of 'directing terrorism'.

The UDA's still legal status was becoming more and more problematic by this time. In 1988, the television reporter Roger Cook used his programme to pose as a businessman handing over substantial protection money to a senior UDA member with concealed cameras running. The recipient received a lengthy prison sentence as a result. Four years later, a Granada Television *World in Action* documentary aired the case for a ban on the UDA, and this was in fact announced by Sir Patrick Mayhew, the Secretary of State for Northern Ireland, in August of 1992.

However, what brought about this decision was a police inquiry into serious allegations of collusion between the UDA and elements of the security forces, particularly the Ulster Defence Regiment. Evidence emerged of photomontages and other details of suspected republicans exchanging hands and a large number of UDA members were arrested and held for questioning. Few were ever charged in the end but their absence on lengthy periods of remand, as well as the August ban on the organisation, made possible what was described by insiders as a slimming down and regrouping into a much tighter cell structure, not far removed, in fact, from the IRA's.

Along with UVF operations the UDA's renewed striking power created real fear among republicans as high profile figures were targeted and killed in increasing numbers. The home of Gerry Adams in West Belfast was identified and attacked but innocent Catholics continued to be victims as in February 1992, when gunmen of the Ulster Freedom Fighters massacred five of them in Sean Graham's betting shop on Belfast's Lower Ormeau Road. This was claimed to be revenge for an IRA ambush at Teebane crossroads in County Tyrone a day or two previously, in which eight Protestant workmen lost their lives when their minibus went over a landmine. 'A Catholic for every Protestant' was the precept which drove UDA actions as it had in the 1970s and it could be implemented with a firepower formidably strengthened by arms purchases from South Africa and elsewhere.

As always in periods of the worst tension in Northern Ireland's conflict, brutal tribalism could reassert itself. In late October 1993 an IRA bomb, supposedly meant for Johnny Adair and the UDA Inner Council, destroyed a fish shop on the Shankill Road and killed nine Protestants. The UDA premises above the shop were empty at the time and it was early on a Saturday afternoon when the pavement outside was crowded with shoppers as the entire building collapsed on them. The attack was a reckless, indiscriminate and barbaric outrage, though this did not deter the IRA from giving the bomber, Sean Begley from Ardoyne, the full honours of a republican funeral. Appalling Loyalist reprisals followed, notably the UFF's Halloween onslaught on a pub at Greysteel near Londonderry, which took seven lives.

Robert Torrens Knight, 24 years old, arriving at court in Limavady 8 November 1993. He was charged and later convicted for his part in the UFF's Halloween massacre of seven people in the Rising Sun bar at Greysteel, a village in County Londonderry. It was a reprisal for the IRA's Shankill Road bomb a week earlier.

Members of the south Belfast brigade of the Ulster Freedom Fighters, fire shots in memory of Brian Morton, who died while handling explosives in the Seymour Hill area, 12 July 1997.

Even at this dark time, London and Dublin were preparing the ground for secret talks with an IRA leadership to whom an unwinnable war had begun to move too close for comfort. Outside the South Armagh area, few IRA attacks were succeeding and many were being aborted due to the role of informers and intensive security forces' surveillance. Amidst many protestations of its foresight and magnanimity, the IRA ceasefire came at the end of August 1994. It had taken them over two decades of killing to arrive at the analysis of Northern Ireland's conflict formulated by the Official Republican movement in 1972.

The UDA was well represented some six weeks later when the Loyalist ceasefire was announced. Among its representatives were John McMichael's son Gary and David Adams, who had worked tenaciously in arguing the case for a Loyalist response to the IRA announcement. Both were active in what had become the Ulster Democratic Party, a reconstitution of the older Ulster Loyalist Democratic Party formed in 1981. As with the UVF's political spokesmen, present at this historic occasion, a hard road lay ahead for them and their hopes that paramilitary Loyalism would put violence behind it in favour of a political road proved to be premature.

UDA members patrol the interface areas of north Belfast
during violent clashes on the peacelines.

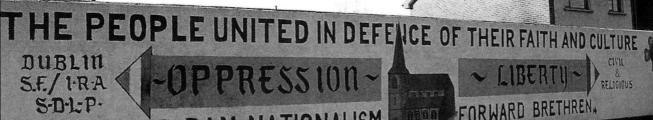

THE PEOPLE UNITED IN DEFENCE OF THEIR FAITH AND CULTURE

DUBLIN
S.F./I·R·A
S·D·L·P·

CIVIL &
RELIGIOUS

~OPPRESSION~   ~LIBERTY~

SMASH PAN-NATIONALISM   FORWARD BRETHREN.

Portadown mural.

WILL MAINTAIN.   OUR MESSAGE TO THE   IRISH IS SIMPLE   WE WILL MAINTA
HANDS OFF ULSTER
OUR NATIONALITY   IRISH OUT
THE ULSTER CONFLICT IS ABOUT NATIONALITY.   OUR FAITH AND OU
NATIONALITY.

'Freedom corner'. UDA mural, lower end of Newtown Road, Belfast.

Billy Wright of the LVF, in front of Drumcree church, Portadown, 7 July 1996.

Ulster Democratic Party posters being put up in Lower Shankill during the 1998 Assembly Elections

Ulster Freedom Fighters mural in Shankill area.

Above: Mural in Bangor.
Right: These images are a break from the usual paramilitary murals.
Each image illustrates a recent Republican set back.

Close-up of 'Freedom Corner'.
A UDA mural on Belfast's Newtownards Road.

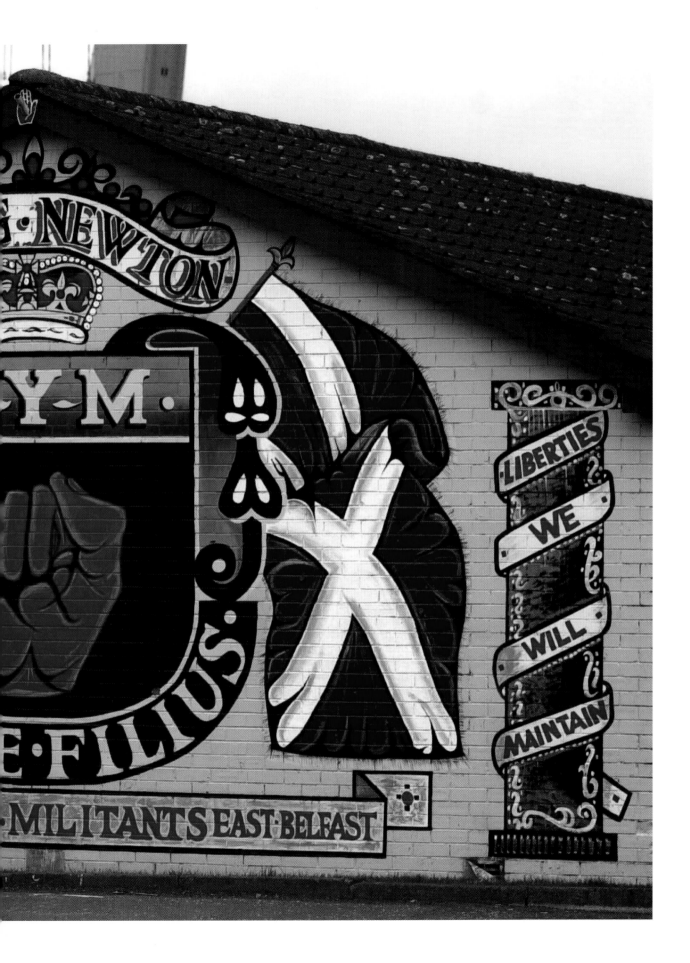

103

UDA mural in Lower Shankill.

· UYM ·
ULSTER YOUNG MILITANTS
TERRAE FILIUS

The UFF issuing a statement. 2001.

CHAPTER FIVE

AFTER THE CEASEFIRES: WAR WITHIN LOYALISM

For quite some time the Loyalist ceasefire held and helped to create some of the space needed for the convoluted politics of the 'peace process' which developed from it and the IRA's own 'cessation' as they liked to call it. However, John Major, a Prime Minister who, with Albert Reynolds, the Irish Taoiseach, had helped to prepare the way for the ceasefires and who may well have regarded peace in Northern Ireland as his passport into history, was unwilling to talk directly to Sinn Fein until the IRA made a move to decommission its weapons.

This angered the IRA but was not the main reason for it going back to war with its bomb attack at Canary Wharf in London on 9 February, 1996. Keeping the movement united was also a major consideration and bombs across the water were a way to achieve this. The priority of the new campaign was to take terror back to English cities while not pursuing anything more than a low level of operations in Northern Ireland itself, though more soldiers and RUC officers were killed there.

Inevitably this reactivated Loyalist suspicions but in late February a statement from the Combined Loyalist Military Command signalled a disinclination by the UVF and UDA to be provoked into premature action, though also a readiness to act when the time was right: 'From a position of confidence, strength and sophistication, we have withstood the recent provocation of IRA bombs on the mainland which have killed our innocent British fellow citizens.

'These atrocities cannot be permitted to continue without a telling response from this source. We are poised and ready to strike to effect. We will give blow for blow. As in the past, whatever the cost we will gladly pay it.'

The tone of this communiqué defined the Loyalist response to an IRA campaign which over the next sixteen months never, by that organisation's own ruthless standards, really moved into top gear. Alongside the question of IRA intentions and how best to read and respond to them, there was a political agenda

A young member of the UFF's West Belfast C Company posing with an AK-47 assault rifle.

for Loyalists to involve themselves in with council elections in 1996 and also votes to be cast for a new constitutional forum set up by the Major government.

The UVF-linked Progressive Unionist Party polled more votes than the Ulster Democratic Party, with Billy Hutchison and David Ervine, both former prisoners, winning seats on Belfast City Council. An electoral pact might well have achieved a better overall result but in both parties vivid memories of hostilities between the UDA and the UVF worked against this. Despite the imperative of fighting the IRA, they had also fought each other, the UVF seeing its much bigger rival as a threat to its power base within the Loyalist community. Control of territory and revenue came into it too and the UDA recently claimed to have had more of its members killed by the UVF than by the IRA. In 1994, they still maintained separate military structures and drank in separate pubs and clubs.

Their differences were also political and these should not be ignored. The UVF has always been more literal in its Unionism than the UDA, flying Union Jacks in areas where it is strong, especially in the months of the marching season, while the UDA tends to favour Ulster standards and, more recently, the Israeli flag, a way of identifying with another people they perceive as being under siege. Initially too, there were many more doubters in the UDA about the IRA's ceasefire and the prospects of real reconciliation and some within its ranks began to refer to the more optimistic UVF, or at any rate its leaders, as the 'peace people'.

What really roused Loyalist anger, however, in the post-ceasefire period, was the old issue of the Loyal orders' right to parade along traditional routes even where the population's religious composition had altered. In the Orange citadel of Portadown, the Garvaghy Road leading from Drumcree Church into the town centre became, from July 1995 onwards, the focal point of a dispute which brought Northern Ireland back to the very edge of the sectarian precipice.

In that month, the RUC reversed its initial decision to block a church parade along this road by Portadown Orange lodges, after some days of tension and violence. In the face of non-violent protest by nationalist people, the parade went ahead with David Trimble and Dr Ian Paisley taking part and rashly claiming it as a great Loyalist victory, for which commemorative medals were actually issued.

Top: Marchers and security forces clash at Drumcree. Below: Members of an accordion band play Christmas carols for the protesters at Drumcree Church in Portadown, 2 December 1998.

Loyalist punishment squad based in Taughmonagh Housing Estate. Republicans have similar squads.

The crisis re-ran itself in much more dangerous form in 1996, after the RUC's Chief Constable, Sir Hugh Annesley, announced a total ban on the parade. This decision too was abandoned as a huge protest built up all over the province in support of the Portadown Orangemen. There was rioting, burning, roadblocks and blockades and, once more, Loyalist gunmen re-emerged from the shadows.

Near Portadown on 7 July, as the second Drumcree crisis came to the boil, they shot dead Michael McGoldrick, a Catholic graduate doing summer work as a taxi driver. This cold-blooded murder was not claimed by any organisation but widely attributed to a local UVF unit acting without the authorisation of its Belfast-based command. They announced at a dramatic press conference, at which their spokesmen were armed and masked, that the killers of Michael McGoldrick would be 'stood down' and their unit disbanded.

This proved to be an ominous development because it brought to prominence Portadown-based Billy Wright, a Loyalist gunman with a ferocious reputation who was linked in many people's minds to some particularly savage killings in Mid-Ulster, and also to that of Michael McGoldrick. Most UVF units supported their leadership but Wright was openly defiant, even when the Combined Loyalist Military Command intervened and ordered him to leave

Northern Ireland by midnight on 1 September, 1996, or be executed.

Wright relied on strong support among many young Portadown Loyalists who idolised him. Big rallies, one attended and addressed by a Democratic Unionist Party MP, increased his confidence and the Loyalist Command failed to make good its threat, even when it became clear that Wright was setting up his own break-away Loyalist Volunteer Force and actively seeking recruits.

Billy Wright was born in Wolverhampton, where his father was working, in 1960, but his parents separated. He was taken into a foster home and had what he always recalled as a happy upbringing in a rural community in County Tyrone, where he had Catholic friends and played Gaelic football. His foster parents were Protestant and the IRA's sustained attacks on their co-religionists, often small farmers serving in the local security forces, drew Wright to paramilitary Loyalism. He joined the UVF and on his own admission, took part in a whole series of operations which killed IRA men but also wholly innocent Catholics.

He also joined Ian Paisley's Free Presbyterian church after a period as a lay preacher, although this gave him no immunity from accusations in the press that he was also dealing in drugs to raise funds for the UVF. One Belfast newspaper

Memorial to the UVF massacre of Catholics in Sean Graham's bookmaker's shop on Belfast's Ormeau Road in February 1992.

nicknamed him 'King Rat' and claimed that he was vying with another of its serial killers, 'The Jackal', or Robin Jackson from the Lurgan area, to be the UVF's 'top gun'.

Wright resented the 'King Rat' tag but it stayed with him as his new recruits embarked on a sequence of savage killings both prior to and after the third Drumcree parade crisis in July of 1997. Jackson made clear his disapproval of Wright's flouting the authority of the UVF and

the Loyalist Command but this had little effect on a man who believed that those under his control were simply carrying on a war which Loyalists should never have called off; Wright went to prison in late 1996, convicted of intimidating a woman witness in a Portadown court case, but he was widely thought to have authorised the brutal killings before and after what had become the predictable annual drama of Drumcree the following year. One eighteen year old victim in the Armagh village of

Johnny Adair before he had shorn his hair and begun intensive body-building .

U·D·A SAD DOG ·F

Graffiti added to Johnny Adair mural after the defeat of his C Company supporters in February 2003 .

Aughalee was Bernadette Martin, shot dead in her bed because she was a Catholic who had a Protestant boyfriend.

Another was James Morgan, a sixteen year old schoolboy from the Castlewellan area in County Down. In late July he was seized by a local gang who had given their allegiance to Wright. They beat him to death, set his body alight with petrol and dumped it in a water-logged pit full of farm animal carcasses.

Wright's own turn, however, came on 27 December, 1997, when, in still disputed circumstances, Irish National Liberation Army prisoners armed with a gun climbed into the Loyalist block at the Maze Prison and killed him with a close-range burst of automatic fire. Portadown's town centre closed down for a huge Loyalist funeral of a man who acquired iconic status in death. Murals depicting him went up within days of his burial and young Loyalists in the town and elsewhere began to adopt cropped hair and closely-trimmed beards in tribute.

His murder came in the midst of a period of intensive talks involving Tony Blair's Labour government and all political parties in Northern Ireland, including Sinn Fein. The spate of killings which came in response to Wright's death could easily have de-railed this delicate process, pre-cisely because the UDA were quickly drawn into them, though without taking overt responsibility.

The first of these 'no claim, no blame' killings took place in a North Belfast pub on New Year's Eve 1997. A Catholic civil servant having a quiet drink was killed by automatic fire and it is widely believed that the killer was one of Johnny Adair's closest lieutenants in his Lower Shankill C Company of the UDA. Henry McDonald and Jim Cusack, in their book on the UVF already referred to, believe that he acted without UDA authorisation.

The organisation's Inner Council failed to discipline him, however, an error as crucial as that of the UVF and the Combined Loyalist Military Command's disinclination, eighteen months earlier, to move against Wright. As UDA killings alternated with those carried out by the LVF, the Secretary of state, Marjorie Mowlam, suspended the UDA-linked Ulster Democratic Party from the political talks at Stormont and the IRA responded by launching two fatal attacks on UDA members.

In late February, the Inner Council halted further killings by its own members, though keepers of the flame lit by Billy Wright went on killing. The all-party Stormont talks survived, the Ulster Democratic Party was allowed to re-join them and in front of the world's media the Belfast Agreement was signed on Good Friday, 1998.

Apart from the sophisticated power-sharing and equality mechanisms it had devised, the

Agreement required both a referendum on its terms followed by elections to a new Assembly. The early summer of 1998 was a period of intense political activism for both the UVF and the UDA. Such spokesmen as David Ervine, Billy Huchison and Gary McMichael gambled heavily on the Agreement's acceptability to a sceptical Loyalist electorate. Old warriors like Andy Tyrie re-entered the fray to press for a 'yes' vote and Michael Stone, the Milltown cemetery killer, used a prison parole to appear at a Loyalist rally in support of the Agreement at the Ulster Hall in Belfast.

The event's organisers claimed not to have known in advance of Stone's unscheduled appearance but he received a tumultuous ovation, just as released IRA prisoners had in Dublin a few days earlier at a Sinn Fein rally.

By no means all of the Protestant electorate cast a 'yes' vote but enough did so to contribute to a seventy per cent majority for the Agreement among those who turned out. Assembly elections followed and gave the UVF a strong voice with the election of Ervine and Hutchison. The UDA's political representatives, who had worked equally hard for the Agreement were left out in the cold, none of them succeeding in winning a seat.

This was an ominous outcome, causing many within the UDA's ranks to ask what they had really gained from a process they began to see being driven by an increasingly Irish nationalist agenda. As ominous was the start of the programme of prisoner releases under the terms of the Belfast Agreement.

UVF prisoners, on the whole, made low-key exits from the Maze and accepted their organisation's cohesive political discipline. With the UDA it was different, because of Johnny Adair. Some UDA leaders like John Gregg, its South East Antrim Brigadier, later said that he had only supported the Agreement to get his friends out of prison, but he had a military concept of organisational discipline and never had the potential or the desire to be a dangerously loose cannon like Adair.

Adair himself was finally released, amidst great celebrations by UDA members in the Maze prison car park in May 1999. He was transformed in appearance, with his head shaved and a physique heavily muscular, not just from 'pumping iron' in the prison gym but from what some fellow prisoners believed had been the addictive use of steroids. It was claimed that some of these had veterinary additives, so Adair, behind his back, became known,

UDA Tigers Bay mural in North Belfast. 10 October 2001.

UDA members fire shots in memory of LVF member Mark 'Swinger' Fulton, in front of a mural of Billy Wright.

especially to prisoners from other areas of Belfast, as 'Mad Cow' rather than 'Mad Dog'.

He had known little in his life except the troubles, running the streets of the Shankill as a teenager involved in petty crime and in a punk rock band of National Front sympathies. He is said, in fact, to have been warned about his behaviour by the local UDA unit prior to being accepted into it in the early 1980s. From then on he did much to create his own legend, once boasting to an Irish journalist as he drove her up the Shankill Road that before her, the only Catholics he had had in his car had been dead ones.

He may not have carried out in person all the killings attributed to him. However, a defendant in a murder trial in 1995, arising from the shooting of a young Protestant in his mid-twenties, although an invalid with the mental age of a 12 year old, did name Adair as the executioner. By then he was acting as if he was a West Belfast Brigadier and even when he went to prison that year, he retained his power base in the West Belfast battalion's C Company on the Lower Shankill. Inside the Maze, he maintained his contacts with ongoing drugs dealing in the area while developing ambitions to play a bigger role within the UDA.

When Adair's release under the terms of the Belfast Agreement fell due in December 1999, tension was rising once more. Using the 'flag of convenience' name 'the Red Hand Defenders' the Portadown-based Loyalist Volunteer Force as well as dissidents within the UDA, stepped up petrol and pipe-bomb attacks on Catholic homes in Belfast and elsewhere. The UVF, though carrying out its share of punishment beatings and shootings in its own areas, viewed these maverick Loyalists with increasing unease, especially after one of their own senior figures, Robert Jamieson, was murdered in Portadown in January 2000.

They took savage revenge the following month, on a teenager who had been seen in Billy Wright's company and a friend with no paramilitary involvement at all. Their bodies, mutilated from knife wounds, were dumped on a country road close to the village of Tandragee not far from Portadown.

By this time, Johnny Adair was being seen in Portadown and was also supervising the painting of new murals on the Lower Shankill in tribute to Billy Wright. Claiming to the media to be 'working for his community', Adair, using his family home on Boundary Way in the Lower Shankill and frequently accompanied by the

A well known female member of the UFF's infamous C-Company. 20 August 2000.

123

The UDA march past a mural depicting a 'British bulldog' chasing a Gerry Adams 'mouse' to Dublin, the Lower Shankill housing estate.

John 'Grugg' Gregg, with the drum, marching in the Rathcoole estate in North Belfast.

more intelligent but manipulative John White, ran the area as if it were his own property. New murals converted it into a lurid Loyalist theme park and drug dealing and under-age drinking flourished while journalists entering his fiefdom were liable to be threatened.

In July, as Orangemen gathered at Drumcree for yet another mobilisation in support of their Portadown brethren's right to parade there, Adair took most of his 'C' Company men as well as his Alsatian dog, Rebel, to join them. All, including the Alsatian, wore teeshirts proclaiming this unit to be 'Simply the Best'.

What led to open hostilities, however, was the UDA's decision to support what it called a celebration of 'Loyalist culture' scheduled for Saturday 20 August. As many as 10,000 UDA men, in combat kit and led by flute bands and masked colour parties, marched at midday up the Shankill Road en route for a rally to take place on open ground close to Johnny Adair's house.

Serious violence, with shots fired, erupted when one group of marchers raised a Loyalist Volunteer Force standard outside the Rex bar, regularly used by the UVF. RUC armoured cars and Mobile Support Units moved in to try and

Johnny Adair, left, celebrating at his welcome home party outside his home, with his wife Gina and John White, in May 2002.

keep control but an open feud was under way which would leave a trail of bodies behind it as old scores were viciously settled. Among the victims were Bobby Mahood, a popular publican and former UVF member, and a friend, Jackie Coulter, a UDA man. Both were anxious to try to halt the violence before it got out of control but were ambushed and shot dead on the Crumlin Road by UVF gunmen.

Adair's re-arrest did not immediately halt the killing. As many as eight hundred people linked by association or simply where they lived to one or other side, were driven from their homes and had to be re-housed, while in an act of symbolic venom, the home of Gusty Spence, within easy walking distance of Johnny Adair's house, was broken into and vandalised.

An Ulster Unionist councillor, Chris McGimpsey, who worked round the clock to help families caught up in this frenzy of violence, spoke of the Shankill having the heart torn out of it by what was happening. It was a justifiable response but other UDA and UVF brigades in the main held back from getting drawn into the killing.

That proved to be impossible two years later when, once more, Johnny Adair was released on licence from Maghaberry prison. By then, the UDA's political wing, the Ulster Democratic Party, had disbanded and the hard core 'military' element within the organisation had never had

much faith in it. Events in 2000 had shown that it had neither the electoral support nor Assembly-level representation to halt the feud. That had been brought about by other intermediaries as well as the UDA and UVF leadership.

In mid-May 2002, Adair returned to the Lower Shankill to address in defiant terms a raucous 'welcome home' party outside his house. C Company, supporters were told, would 'retake' the Shankill from the UVF and other 'rotten Prods'. It soon became clear that his agenda was also to oust from positions of command within the UDA men who might not do his bidding.

UDA history should have told him that this might be a high risk strategy. Within weeks of his release, the UDA's Inner Council agreed to appoint a new brigadier in North Belfast, Andre Shoukri, known because of his parentage as 'the Egyptian' although he had lived all his life in the city. He, however, proved to be only a temporary ally. Within the UDA it was common knowledge that Adair also wanted to have removed from his command the East Belfast Brigadier Jim Gray, nicknamed 'Doris Day' for his bleached blond hair and liking for highly coloured floral shirts.

When in September 2002 Steven Warnock, a drug dealer with LVF connections, was shot dead, Adair blamed Gray and demanded action

Mural honouring Jackie Coulter a member of the UDA, shot dead by UVF gunmen, during the Loyalist fued in the summer of 2000.

Scene of the murder of John Gregg.

The Funeral of John Gregg.

against him from the Inner Council. However, Adair and his LVF allies refused to wait for their decision and within days, Gray himself was shot, sustaining facial injuries but surviving the attack. It was in fact the UVF who shot Warnock but Adair continued to blame the UDA's East Belfast brigade. In defiance of an Inner Council order, he attended Warnock's funeral along with John White.

For this and other offences, including unauthorised contacts with Sinn Fein as well as with the LVF, Adair and White were expelled from the UDA within days of Warnock's funeral. A vicious trial of strength followed in which the homes of mainstream UDA supporters were bombed and shot at, while threats and intimidation led others living close to Adair to vacate their homes. Two further killings resulted, in late December and early January, but it began to be clear that Adair and White were losing support. The other companies of the UDA's West Belfast Second Battalion refused to back them and former allies like Shoukri declared their support for the Inner Council.

Adair was re-arrested but continued to give orders to his dwindling band of adherents from his cell on Maghaberry prison's isolation block. The final proof of his and White's loss of touch with reality, however, was the murder on Saturday, 1 February, 2003, of John 'Grugg' Gregg, Brigadier in command of the UDA's largest area, South East Antrim, which extends from the Rathcoole housing estate in North Belfast as far as Carrickfergus and Larne.

Here, after a series of murders in which most, though not all the victims were Catholics, the Loyalist ceasefire no longer meant a great deal. Much of the responsibility for this violence was attributed to Gregg by both the media and the security forces. He was a physically formidable figure, his upper body tattooed with Loyalist emblems and an image of the Grim Reaper. He was also a Loyalist hero for his part in an almost successful attempt on the life of Gerry Adams in 1984. This earned him a lengthy prison sentence but also guaranteed him senior rank in the UDA on his release.

Along with another UDA man, Gregg was shot dead in a taxi, minutes after leaving the evening Stranraer to Belfast ferry after having been to Glasgow for a Rangers match. He was the most senior UDA man to be murdered since John McMichael more than fifteen years before. His killing, widely believed to have been authorised by Adair, was an affront which the Inner Council of the UDA could not ignore.

Gregg himself, not long before his own death, had assured the media that retribution for the Adair faction was imminent and said the same to this author in an interview in December of 2002. Ahead of his funeral, the UDA let rumours circulate that it was going to organise a mass march into the Lower Shankill to root out Adair's remaining supporters. This was a

Jackie McDonald, left, south Belfast UDA brigadier .

ruse. Boundary Way, the street where Adair and his family lived and where John White had set up a small office for press briefings, was invaded late on the evening of Wednesday, 5 February by over a hundred UDA men, a large number of them armed.

Many C Company members had already prudently made the journey a short distance from the Shankill Road to a UDA social club in Heather Street, to affirm their loyalty to the Inner Council. Those who remained were out-numbered in the fracas which followed. Windows were smashed, doors kicked in and identified Adair associates beaten up. Police and troops arrived to restore order but by then Adair's wife Gina and her family, along with White and around twenty supporters, had been told to get out of Northern Ireland.

They were last seen leaving the Lower Shankill under a strong police escort which accompanied them to the ferry for Scotland. They arrived at the port of Cairnryan at around 4.30 in the morning, with only a few belongings, although there were unconfirmed reports than Gina Adair was found by Scottish police to be carrying a very large sum of money.

Later that morning, UDA men returned to Boundary Way with cans of paint to deface some of the huge murals put up at Adair's orders. They then travelled four miles to Rathcoole to join the huge turn out for John Gregg's funeral. Symbolic shots were fired over his coffin and he was later buried in the uniform of the Cloughfern Young Conquerors flute band, in which he and his teenage son had both played.

Gregg's murder is now known to have post-poned a new initiative by the UDA's leadership which was announced to a press conference two weeks after his funeral. The organisation's brigadiers absented themselves and political spokesmen on behalf of the Ulster Political Research Group, including two Belfast Councillors, handled the occasion. 'As from 21 February 2003' they told the assembled press 'all units of the Ulster Freedom Fighters, the Ulster Defence Association and the Ulster Young Militants in mainland Britain and Northern Ireland have begun to observe a twelve month period of military inactivity.'

The statement stressed that the UDA's Inner Council would retreat from a public role and that 'the entire organisation will become face-less once again'. An apology was offered for 'personal use or any other involvement' in illegal drugs by UDA members. A pledge was also made that the organisation would urge Loyalists to leave the defence of their areas to the new Police Service of Northern Ireland. Dialogue with either Sinn Fein or the IRA was rejected and the declaration, which was named after John Gregg, finished with the words 'the Ulster Defence Association will as always be the last line of defence'. This was widely seen as a signal that the UDA's military structure was to remain in tact.

CHAPTER SIX

THE LOYALIST FUTURE: AN OLD CONFLICT IN A NEW CENTURY

Both THE UDA and the UVF remain intact and powerful organisations in Northern Ireland while the smaller Loyalist Volunteer Force still has a network of support in Portadown, Lurgan and parts of North Belfast. The LVF remain well-armed although in 1998 they did offer up some token weapons for de-commissioning under the auspices of General John De Chastelain, who was appointed by the British government to monitor the process of paramilitary disarming under the terms of the Belfast Agreement.

In Belfast the UDA and the UVF still have the ability both to orchestrate and control and even to halt street violence which in recent years has been recurrent at some of the city's sectarian interface areas. The UDA in particular was blamed for some of the scenes which were shown on television screens around the world in 2001 and 2002 outside the Holy Cross Girls' Primary School in Ardoyne, North Belfast. This area, though it was not always so, has become predominantly nationalist and Catholic during the years of the troubles and was widely thought of by the security forces as an IRA stronghold.

A small Protestant population has however remained in Glenbryn at the upper end of Ardoyne Road just across from Alliance Avenue. It is here that the Holy Cross school stands and during a tense summer in 2001, it became the target of angry picketing by Glenbryn Protestants who claimed they were being taunted and jostled on the pavement by some Catholic parents taking their children to the school. There were other allegations of an attack on a local man tying Loyalist bunting to a lamppost in the street and of the desecration of a street memorial to a local taxi driver murdered by the IRA.

The protest built up into a protracted and vicious confrontation over many months which required a substantial army and police presence to guarantee access to the school for those parents, by no means all of them, who wanted their children to reach the school by the Ardoyne Road entrance. Parents, pupils and two local priests who nearly always accompanied them, were abused verbally, spat upon and attacked with missiles. On one occasion these included a blast bomb which exploded not far from the pupils. This led Billy

Masked UDA men on parade.

137

Hutchison, a witness, to tell the media that he 'was ashamed to be a Protestant.'

He was in attendance as an observer on that occasion and denied UVF involvement in the violence. Republicans claimed, though, that since the Loyalist feud on the Shankill the previous year, some UDA men had moved into Glenbryn in order to whip up violence against the nearby Catholic community. John White was seen more than once with the Protestant protesters but stated he was there to monitor the situation and that he did not want to see UDA involvement. Not everyone believed him but others in the organisation viewed the whole episode as a disaster for the image of Loyalism and took no part in it, claiming that the Glenbryn Protestants had walked into a trap set for them.

The venom of this dispute, incomprehensible to most people in England, was of course a product of fear and hatred which had festered over many years but it was also a result of major demographic change in North Belfast. The magnitude of this is clear in the Northern Ireland Census finally published in late 2002. This shows how areas like Glenbryn now lie almost surrounded by a fast-growing nationalist population which they believe wants all the area's housing for itself.

Given the recent and awful history of former Yugoslavia, the term 'ethnic cleansing' might seem an extravagant one to use in the context of Northern Ireland but it has begun to be used in a magazine like Combat, published by the Ulster Volunteer Force. It featured in their

response to events only five or six miles away in East Belfast in the spring and summer of 2002 when serious violence erupted in the mainly nationalist Short Strand area.

This small and self-contained community lies at the edge of solidly Loyalist neighbourhoods and it was here, in the grounds of St Matthew's Parish Church, that the Provisional IRA fought its first major gun battle in June 1970 when the Short Strand came under sustained attack. In 2002, tensions were rising over scheduled Orange Order parades in the area, though none of these went through the Short Strand itself. The area's residents had to shop and visit a doctor's surgery on the Loyalist Newtonards and Albert Bridge roads. Sectarian clashes followed, then a series of prolonged attacks on the Short Strand itself. The UDA was not directly involved, being preoccupied with internal leadership problems in its East Belfast brigade area, but Short Strand people claimed to have identified known UVF members during riots and attacks on their homes.

IRA gunmen opened fire more than once from the rooftops of the Short Strand and petrol bombs and missiles from the area almost destroyed Cluan Place, a small group of Protestant homes opening off the Albert Bridge Road and divided from the Short Strand by a security wall. Combat, in its summer issue, used some dramatic photographs and reports to claim that republicans were 'talking up' attacks on their locality in order to justify a deliberate attempt to force out a few vulnerable Protestants. 'This is a deliberate development to Republican strategy,' Combat wrote, 'slowly

Members of the Independent International Commission on Decommissioning destroy some of the terrorists weapons which were handed over by the LVF in Belfast, 18 December 1998.

but surely they are drawing more and more Loyalist areas into a state of desperate defence. Men and women of these areas do not want to be in the streets fighting tooth and nail for survival but it is a necessity forced upon them by shady individuals hell-bent on the eradication of the Protestant race in Ulster.'

Fears as deep as these will continue to provide support for the Loyalist paramilitary organisations in Belfast and Derry while in solidly Protestant towns like Larne, Carrickfergus and Ballymena, any increase in the Catholic population is viewed with suspicion by some, particularly in the UDA in Larne's case, where intensified pipe and petrol bomb attacks on Catholic homes have been taking place since the signing of the Belfast Agreement. The long-delayed publication of the Northern Ireland Census in December 2002 has not yet allayed these fears even though it revealed a clear majority of a now enlarged population which supports the Union.

Some older members of the UDA have come to see continued communal violence for the destructive blind alley that it is. Sammy Duddy, who joined the organisation in its early days and went on to make his talents available to it as an illustrator, cartoonist and editor of some of its publications, now does political work for it from its North Belfast office and invests much effort in keeping young Protestants from Tiger Bay and North Queen street away from interface confrontations with Catholics from the New Lodge area.

He does much of his work through the Ulster Political Research group which announced the UDA's February 2003 ceasefire and he is also involved with the Loyalist Commission, a body set up after the 2000 feud. Its role is to bring together paramilitaries, politicians and Protestant clergy so that they can together address the problems and fears of Protestant communities. It has also met senior ministers from the Northern Ireland Office for extended discussions.

The Commission's credibility and perhaps its potential for greater influence in Loyalist areas was significantly strengthened when it was able to persuade the Glenbryn Protestant

community not to make a paramilitary response to the Holy Cross school crisis and to settle instead for negotiations both with the nationalist residents of Ardoyne as well as with the Northern Ireland Office. Also as a result of these talks, CCTV cameras were installed in Glenbryn and the level of regular policing improved there.

One Loyalist close to the Commission's work declared: 'We started by trying to patch up differences between Loyalists but now we're into something much more constructive, something that could wean people away from paramilitary violence and put respect and morale back into these areas.'

This could indeed be a new and hopeful road for paramilitary Loyalists to travel but decades of conflict which, prior to the break-up of the Soviet Union and former Yugoslavia turned Northern Ireland into Europe's worst killing ground since the Second World War have left deep wounds which will take years to heal. They also drew many Loyalists into the insidious business of large-scale fund-raising through protection operations, illegal drinking clubs and more recently, drug dealing. Some of these were central figures in the most recent power struggle within the UDA.

The return to prison of Johnny Adair in January of 2003 and the departure from Northern Ireland a few weeks later of many of those close to him, has not resolved the problem, as the UDA's spokesmen in fact admitted in their February ceasefire statement. Much must now depend on whether it will feel able or willing to co-operate with the new Assets Recovery Agency. Its head is a former Deputy Chief Constable of the RUC and it has powers, modelled on the Irish Republic's Criminal Assets bureau, to force suspected criminals and racketeers to declare their sources of income on pain of imprisonment if they refuse.

Officers in all of Northern Ireland's twenty nine police divisions will work in contact with the new agency and in March 2003, it announced that it had a 'top twelve' list of targets for investigation. Not all of these will necessarily be Loyalists. Present and former IRA members are also widely thought to be involved in hugely lucrative cross-border fuel and cigarette smuggling, pirate drink, perfume and video production, as well as drug dealing.

If this agency really is given the resources to make its investigations effective and to make a reality of its powers of enforcement, much more will gradually come to light about the history of Northern Ireland's troubles and the role in these of the paramilitary Loyalist organisations which are the subject of this book.

So, too, may at least some of the truth start to emerge about the relationship of the British state to the Loyalists' war in what they claimed was the defence of their community against the republican enemy. Rumours and conjecture about this have persisted for a very long time and indeed date right back to the start of the troubles

In August 1974, a serving army officer who concealed his real name contributed an article to Monday World, then the journal of the right-wing Conservative Monday Club. He gave an overview of the army's role, five years into the troubles, and recalled how a Loyalist backlash against Civil Rights and the IRA confronted the army with the possibility of a war on two fronts.

'This it got with the rise of the UDA,' he wrote, and went on to call it 'a paramilitary manifestation of the growing fear of the Protestant working class that it was being sold down the river by Whitehall. In order to combat this threat, the army chose quite deliberately to give the UDA tacit support. The UDA virtually ran East and North Belfast. It was the threat of UDA intervention that led to Motorman (the codename for the August 1972 operation by the army to end IRA 'no go' areas) and it was the threat of UDA action against the Catholic ghettoes in Belfast that led to even higher troop levels. Almost too late, in the winter of 1972, the Army realised that it had assisted in the birth of a monster. It sought to act but was only able to cage the beast, the secret of its destruction was lost with its birth.'

How far in reality 'the beast was caged' has been much debated and there are those, particularly Republicans, who believe that from a British point of view, the creature continued to have its uses. This appears to have been the view of the late Alan Clark when he was serving as Minister of State for Defence in John Major's government. He visited Northern

Ireland in January 1991 and confided his predictably pessimistic thoughts about the situation there to his diary: 'the general atmosphere is bleak, overlaid with the oppression of terror; deep and perpetual feuds, suspicion and callousness. I am confirmed in my opinion that it is hopeless here. All we can do is arm the Orangemen – to the teeth – and get out.'

By Orangemen, he of course meant the Loyalists more generally and by 1991 some commentators were of the opinion that British undercover and intelligence services were, if not arming them, already acting in collusion with some of the paramilitaries. A series of killings by Loyalists had fuelled this belief within much of the nationalist community, in particular that of Patrick Finucane, a well-known Catholic solicitor. On 12 February 1989, he was shot dead at his home in North Belfast while eating an evening meal with his wife and children.

Finucane had been a skilful and tenacious defence lawyer, acting often, though not exclusively, in cases involving clients with alleged IRA connections. Three of his brothers were active members of the IRA and one is reputed to have risen as high as its Army Council. Lawyers, magistrates and judges were often assassination targets during the troubles and the IRA had already killed several of them before the Finucane murder.

The circumstances of his death, however, have since been at the heart of allegations that members of a highly secret British Army unit, the Force Research Unit, had acted with the UDA which, using the cover name of the Ulster Freedom Fighters, was quick to claim responsibility for Pat Finucane's killing. New evidence, which was not made public, was passed early in 2003 to the Director of Public Prosecutions in Northern Ireland by Sir John Stevens, head of the London Metropolitan Police and entrusted by the British government with undertaking a full investigation into the case.

Among those questioned by the Stevens enquiry team was Brigadier Gordon Kerr, a British officer who commanded the Force Research Unit in the late 1980s. He was subsequently appointed to be military attaché in Beijing and then assigned to special intelligence work in the Middle East. After questioning by the Stevens team, there were rumours that Kerr might face major charges, though this has not yet happened.

Such charges would relate to the claim that several UDA men involved in planning and carrying out Finucane's murder were in fact working either for army intelligence, including the Force Research Unit, or the RUC's Special Branch. In January 2003, Stevens confirmed that most of those arrested and questioned had indeed worked for one or other of these agencies and that they nearly all belonged to C Company of the UDA's West Belfast battalion. This was the unit controlled by Johnny Adair which was at the centre of the brutal Loyalist

Steven McKeague on the far left, circa 1994, with other UDA members. Many of the killings carried out by C Company of the West Belfast Battalion of The Ulster Freedom Fighters, have been attributed to him.

power struggle already described in this book. Thus far, three names have emerged: Brian Nelson, William Stobie and Ken Barrett. Nelson, an ex-soldier, was recruited by the FRU and at the same time rose to the position of Chief Intelligence Officer in the UDA, with the responsibility for running a database on prospective targets for assassination. Among them was Pat Finucane, but there were many more. Stobie had access to C Company's weapons and provided a gun, stolen from an army base, which was used to kill the lawyer. In December 2001, Barrett fled Belfast after talking to the RUC.

He was believed to have accepted special police protection 'somewhere in England' but later took part in a BBC television programme in which he claimed that he personally had killed Pat Finucane. Some UDA insiders queried this claim, while many nationalists and human rights campaigners raised the question of whether the intelligence services declined to act on the information provided by Nelson on the planned murder. They, with some support from within the media, have also claimed that the FRU and Special Branch allowed a whole series of other killings to go ahead in order to protect their UDA informers.

Army and police intelligence also, it should be reiterated, had highly placed informers to protect within the IRA whose information was even more vital but in 1989, the first Stevens inquiry into allegations of security force collusion with Loyalists led to Nelson being arrested and charged with a number of murders. When he stood trial at Belfast Crown Court in 1992, Brigadier Kerr, then a Colonel, appeared as a character witness for him, praising Nelson's courage and stressing the number of lives he had saved including, he claimed, that of Gerry Adams. When questioned later about this evidence, in January 2003, Sir John Stevens went on record with the view that Kerr's testimony had been inaccurate. Nelson, however, was allowed to make a plea of guilty to lesser charges and received what was widely seen as a lenient ten year sentence, which he served in England. In 2001, William Stobie went on trial on charges of conspiracy to murder, only for the case to collapse when a key witness refused to testify. He was released but had already talked too much to the police for his own good and was shot dead just a few weeks later.

At the time of writing, the Stevens inquiry is continuing. Over a fourteen year period, Sir John's officers have interviewed 15,000 people and amassed a huge dossier of evidence on the case. The Finucane family and their supporters believe it will not now lead to convictions or to revealing the truth and in April 2002, the British government asked a retired Canadian judge to look into the Finucane case, as well as five other highly controversial murders.

All this has been part of what the Irish journalist Martin Dillon described as the 'dirty war' in the title of one of his books on the conflict in Northern Ireland. He included the IRA's war in that description, it should be added, but republicans are always keen to pre-judge the issue of collusion between the security forces and Loyalist paramilitary bodies. If collusion was as structured a policy as they claim, sanctioned at the very highest levels of government, the six small counties of Northern Ireland would hold infinitely more IRA graves and burial plots and the IRA leaders might have been brought to the negotiating table very much sooner than they were.

Their 'long war' in the end brought them only to a partitionist settlement which, under the terms of the Belfast Agreement, upholds the principle of Northern Ireland's union with Britain by majority consent. Irish unification, despite the various cross-border mechanisms set up by the Agreement, remains a long way down the road, something clearly reinforced by the 2002 Census findings.

Many Northern Ireland Protestants now have a very different perception of the Irish Republic from that of their parents and grandparents. It may not be a secular state on the model of other functioning democracies and it has lost most of its Protestant population since independence: but equally, it is no longer the Catholic-dominated state or society which it was within living memory and from which such a talented writer as Edna O'Brien was glad to escape.

The Irish economy is now a vibrant one, well integrated within the European Union which has contributed hugely to its growth. This has helped Irish society to become outward-looking and ready to re-examine old certainties. In the referendum on the Belfast Agreement in 1998, not only did a clear majority of citizens vote for it, they also voted away their 1937 Constitution's Articles 2 and 3, with their admittedly only legalistic but still symbolic claim to jurisdiction over the northern counties as part of the 'national territory'.

Ulster Loyalists remain alert to whatever residues of anti-British feeling may linger within Irish political and cultural life and they continue to resent Irish neutrality in the Second World War without necessarily grasping all the complexities involved in it. Even so, hardline Loyalists who have been active in either the UDA or UVF who have visited Dublin will often now admit that they feel under no real threat when they cross the border. Yet they still have to be persuaded that peace in their own northern mini-state is secure and under no danger from either the IRA or its wellwishers in the Republic. Until they can be, the organisations under discussion in this book are likely to remain in existence.

For those who have both killed and put their own lives at risk for the cause of their Ulster, the real border may now lie in Belfast itself. Some of them, though, would like to cross it. One ex-UVF gunmen and long-term prisoner told the writer and broadcaster Peter Taylor in 1999 that what he really looked forward to was the chance to drink a pint in a pub on Belfast's Falls Road. That is surely a modest but eminently worthwhile ambition.

UFF mural in the Lower Shankill Road estate when it was the stronghold of Johnny Adair's C Company UFF West Belfast battalion.

Longer than a cocktail.

SMOKING KIL

A dramatic moment caught by North Belfast News photographer, Thomas McMullan, when an army bomb disposal team diffused a hoax Loyalist van bomb left in the Nationalist Ardoyne district by UDA C Company members. Scenes like this are a reminder to many in Northern Ireland of what the failure of the 'Peace Process' could mean.

UDA Mural.